Have Faith

Sustaining the Spirit for Confirmation and Beyond

A Candidate and
Sponsor Resource

MICHAEL CAROTTA

TWENTY
THIRD 23rd
PUBLICATIONS

Seventh printing 2011

TWENTY-THIRD PUBLICATIONS
A Division of Bayard
One Montauk Avenue, Suite 200
P.O. Box 6015
New London, CT 06320
(860) 437-3012
(800) 321-0411
www.23rdpublications.com

ISBN 978-1-58595-604-3
Library of Congress Catalog Card Number: 2006927962
Printed in the U.S.A.

Credits

The material in Part One regarding vocational callings and seasons, and the practices of Keeping Company, Collecting Moments of Grace, and Confession were gleaned from *Sustaining the Spirit: Callings, Commitments, and Vocational Challenge*, by Catherine Cronin Carotta and Michael Carotta (Twenty-Third Publications, 2005).

The information in How Catholics Are Unique is original material. A more thorough explanation about the distinguishing characteristics of Catholicism can be found in books such as *What Makes Us Catholic: Eight Gifts for Life*, by Thomas H. Groome (Harper San Francisco, 2003).

The characteristics of a young Catholic disciple were adapted from *The Challenge of Adolescent Catechesis: Maturing in Faith*, developed by The National Federation for Catholic Youth Ministry (1986).

The Mitzvot material was adapted from the personal Bar Mitvah journal of Nathaniel Schreiber as shared by his parents John and Rebecca Schreiber. A more thorough explanation of mitzvot can be found in numerous books such as *Doing Mitzvot*, by Rabbi Ronald H. Isaacs and Rabbi Kerry M. Olitzky (KTAV Publishing House, 1994).

A fuller exploration of Taking Heart can be found in *Leadership on the Line*, by R. Heifetz and M. Linsky (Harvard Business School Press, 2002).

The TAPP method of praying and the practice of Honoring the Body first appeared in *Catholic and Capable*, published by Resources for Christian Living (1997). Used with permission. Additional skills for spiritual growth can be found in *Nurturing the Spiritual Life of Your Adolescent*, published by Harcourt Religion (2002).

The practice of Attending to Stories was gleaned from *Sometimes We Dance, Sometimes We Wrestle: Embracing the Spirituality of Adolescent*, published by Harcourt Religion (2002).

Contents

Welcome

You probably already know that Confirmation initiates you into the Catholic Church and into the "fullness of the Holy Spirit." The process you are about to begin will help you take the final steps in your Confirmation preparation. It will prepare you to sustain the spirit for the sacrament of Confirmation and beyond.

This is not a book you just open up and read—it's a book that you *do*. The process will take a few months. It contains self-evaluations, exercises, brief essays, stories, and interviews. It even invites you to do a little research.

The adult you have chosen as your sponsor will be doing the same things you are doing. Choose someone who has faith and who seems to be trying to live it. Choose a sponsor who is easy to talk to. Your sponsor won't have to come to any meetings, so you are free to choose anyone from any part of the country.

There are three parts to this process. After you complete each part, you will find suggested topics that you can discuss with your sponsor. On three different occasions, you and your sponsor can compare a few notes over the phone, via email, or face to face. When you connect with your sponsor, the two of you are only expected to discuss the specific topics listed. The rest of the material is for your own personal reflection.

The person coordinating your parish Confirmation program will probably schedule a one-time gathering and invite you and all the other candidates to attend. This will be a time to further discuss some of the topics in this book and perhaps deal with some of the deeper questions the exercises raise. It also gives your program leader an opportunity to touch base with you.

If you take this process seriously, you will discover the strengths and weaknesses of your own spirituality and you will be able to design your own personal Spiritual Growth Plan. What goes into this plan will be entirely up to you. The whole point is to help you nurture your spiritual sense as you deal with the complexities of your life.

At different times in this book, you'll be invited to go to www.spiritandsong.com/compositions. Here you can listen to music that will add a prayerful insight to some of these exercises.

Note to sponsors

This process is meant to be an opportunity for spiritual growth for both you and the candidate. While the book is addressed to the candidate, a substantial amount of the content and exercises have actually been adapted from adult resources. Your participation in this process requires that you complete *all* of the same exercises as the candidate, and that you share your thoughts around the specific topics listed after each of the book's three parts. So please plan on scheduling three conversations—by phone, email, or in person—with the young person who has asked you to be her or his sponsor.

Thank you for willingness to join your candidate as he or she prepares for Confirmation. May this book be the catalyst for further conversations with your candidate in years to come.

PART ONE

The Spiritual Life

In this section you will learn about three dimensions of spirituality and discover the dimension that is most natural to you. You will also explore the "callings" of your life and begin to make a plan for how you can continue to take control of your own spiritual growth. One of the goals of this book is to help you learn enough about your spirituality so that you can create your own Spiritual Growth Plan (SGP). So, the first thing to do is recognize the three different dimensions of spirituality—vertical, horizontal, and internal—then figure out which dimension you are naturally drawn to.

My Spiritual Life Profile

To begin this process, take the following self-assesment survey. On a scale of 1–5, indicate how true each of these statements is for you. 1 equals "not true"; 5 equals "very true." (Note: not everything is supposed to be "very true" for you. Answer honestly so you can get a true picture of your spirituality.)

___ 1.   The most important thing about my faith is keeping close to God.

___ 2.   The most important thing about my faith is being a good person.

___ 3.   The most important thing about my faith is that it helps me cope with life's ups and downs.

___ 4.   My faith motivates me to serve others.

___ 5.   My faith brings me a lot of inner peace.

___ 6.   I pray a lot, and prayer helps me feel closer to God.

___ 7.   My faith helps me feel better when I am sad.

___ 8.   Because of my faith, I try hard to be straight with people.

___ 9.   For me, going to church is an important way to stay close to God.

___ 10. God and I are close.

___ 11. My faith guides my decisions about what's right and wrong.

___ 12. My faith helps me stay hopeful.

___ 13. Because of my faith, I pay attention to when others need help.

___ 14. My faith helps me heal from emotional hurts.

___ 15. Nothing is more important to me than my friendship with God.

___ 16. My faith brings me a lot of happiness.

___ 17. I have a strong relationship with Jesus as my friend and savior.

___ 18. Living in a loving way is the most important thing about my faith.

___ 19. Because of my faith, I believe that it is wrong to tell racist or dirty jokes.

___ 20. My faith helps me deal with my anger.

___ 21. I'm always interested in learning more about God.

Score profile (vertical, horizontal, internal)

Vertical: Add up the numbers you gave for statements
#1, #6, #9, #10, #15, #17, #21
Your vertical score is_____

Horizontal: Add up the numbers you gave for statements
#2, #4, #8, #11, #13, #18, #19
Your horizontal score is_____

Internal: Add up the numbers you gave for statements
#3, #5, #7, #12, #14, #16, #20
Your internal score is_____

• Go to www.spiritandsong.com/compositions/68111 and listen to "Dangerous Wonder" to see what it says about your spiritual potential.

What the survey means

The vertical dimension of spirituality represents the relationship you have between yourself and God "above." The "above" part is why we call it "vertical" (even though God is in others and inside ourselves as well). People with a highly vertical spirituality invest most of their spiritual effort on improving or maintaining their relationship with God by praying regularly, going to church, learning more about God, and/or participating in religious events, rituals, and traditions.

The horizontal dimension of spirituality represents the way your faith motivates you to treat other people. People with a highly horizontal dimension to their spirituality invest most of their spiritual effort trying to be a good person to others. People with a highly horizontal spirituality are always recognizing others in need, helping out, treating people with respect and kindness, and sticking up for those who need it. And they are actively forming a strong moral conscience about what's right and wrong, what's noble and true.

The internal dimension of spirituality represents the way your faith helps you deal with the stuff inside. People with a highly internal dimension invest most of their spiritual effort in coping with emotional issues, past hurts, and life's ups and downs. People with a strong internal dimension often have hope even when things don't go well. They don't give up easily, and they calm down more quickly when they get frustrated or angry.

The goal for true spiritual growth involves the development of all three of these dimensions. This book will help you develop a plan for growing in all three dimensions.

What is spirituality?

Spirituality is about prayer and worship (vertical), but it's more than that. If you spend all your spiritual focus on prayer and worship, you might have a solid personal relationship with God, but you might not be spiritually motivated to serve others.

Spirituality is also about treating others lovingly, making good moral decisions, and being a person of character and conscience (horizontal). But it's more than just that. If you spend all your spiritual focus on others, you will be a kind person but not necessarily someone who maintains a close relationship with God, your soul's truest friend.

Spirituality is also about tapping into your inner strength to handle the emotional issues you struggle with (internal). But it's more than just that, too. If that's all you work on spiritually, you might cope pretty well with life's ups and downs, but you won't necessarily reach out to help others or develop your relationship with God.

These three dimensions are a lot like the three virtues of faith, hope, and love. They each have their primary direction and they each overlap. Faith, hope, and love: vertical, internal, and horizontal. Spiritual growth should take place in all three dimensions. Remember the words of St. Paul: "In the end there are three things that last: faith, hope, and love" (1 Cor 13:13).

- Which of the three dimensions—vertical, horizontal, or internal—represents your strongest spiritual tendencies? Why do you say so?

Seeing three dimensions

Here are some actual statements people have made about their spirituality. Read each one and decide which dimension it represents. Place an "H," "V," or "I" next to each statement.

_____ "I pray a lot, like when I'm waiting for the school bus every morning. I see the changes of the four seasons and I wonder how anyone could think that nature works by accident."

_____ "My faith helps me deal with issues."

_____ "My faith helps me accept everyone, no matter what they wear, what they listen to, or who they hang around with."

_____ "The closest I've been to God in the last six months? Okay, last April I guess. I was stressing out big time, losing weight, always tired but could never fall asleep at night, about to cry over everything—over nothing. My PSAT scores were down. I had a C- in English, baseball was a bust; I couldn't hit anything. And my parents were on me to clean my room, but I never had time and I didn't even know where to start. One night I was listening to music and talking to God—and God started talking back—not like in a real voice, but I was sure it was God talking to me, telling me, 'It will all work out. I'm gonna help you get through this.' I was so sure it was God talking to me. I fell asleep on the top of my bed with all my

Spiritual Dimensions and the Ten Commandments

Practice recognizing the three dimensions of the spiritual life by focusing on the Ten Commandments. We believe that God gave these commandments to Moses, who then gave them to the rest of us. They are the basis or foundation of a universal code of conduct. Almost every other religion in the world has a set of commandments like these. The ancient emperor Hammurabi, who lived before Moses, is said to have had one of the earliest lists of commandments. (Go online to Wikipedia and look up "The Code of Hammurabi," a real code!)

Look up the Ten Commandments in the Bible in the book of Deuteronomy, chapter 5, verses 1–21. Decide which commandments point toward the vertical dimension of spirituality, which point toward the horizontal, and which point to the internal. Place a "V," "H," or "I" after each number below.

1.___ 2.___ 3.___ 4.___ 5.___ 6.___ 7.___ 8.___ 9.___ 10.___

Notice anything?

clothes on. The next day I went to school and quit stressing. Since then, things just began to work out."

"During spring break I did Habitat for Humanity with
some friends in my class, helping this family build their
own home. There was just this mom and her five
daughters. The oldest daughter was fourteen. The mom
worked second shift and had to take the last bus home
just before midnight every night. So it was the oldest
daughter who had to make sure her sisters did their
homework, took baths, and had their clothes laid out
for school. I could never have done that at fourteen!
Such a hard-working family! For the first time in my
life, I understood that being poor is not something people bring on themselves. I really felt like I was doing
something that would make God happy."

"I went on a retreat last month and everyone was in
small groups for the whole time. On the last night, each
small group had to spend an hour of quiet time in the
chapel. It was cool. All dark and all, just the candles lit
and one small light. Since we don't have kneelers in my
church, I decided to kneel. I started looking at the tabernacle and talking to God and got into the zone. God
and I were talking about everything. I forgot that there
were other people in the chapel with me. I knelt for the
whole hour and it felt like fifteen minutes. Talked about
everything. Totally in the zone."

"I ask a lot of questions about God and religion. You
can ask my friends; they'll tell you that I drive them
crazy. But I can't help it. I like learning about religion,
especially my religion."

"Because of my faith, I think it's wrong to tell racist
jokes, stereotype people, or even ignore people who are
different. What God wants most from me, I think, is to
be a good person."

_____ "My faith helps me accept myself even though I'm not as popular as…, as smart as…, as funny as…, or as good looking as…."

_____ "I don't believe in having sex before marriage; it's against my faith. For that matter, so is doing drugs."

_____ "My faith challenges me to use my potential."

Three vocational "callings"

The spiritual life also involves "callings." Seems like everyone wants to know, "What am I called to do with my life?" or "What's my vocation in life?" Usually you ask this sort of question when you think about what career to pursue or which job to take. But questions about callings also have a soulful side because of where the call is coming from—as in, Who is calling you? It helps to see that there are three calling" in life.

1. The call of faith

This is our highest and most basic calling and it addresses the question: "How am I to live?" This call, for all people—Christian, Muslim, Jew, Hindu—is a call to live as a child of God. Ideally, we are invited to make a three-dimensional response to this call: vertical, horizontal, and internal (which you have just reviewed).

2. The call of relationships

This call addresses the question: "With whom am I to live?" and invites us to travel life's journey as a family member, friend, or spouse. Right now, the call of relationships for you is all about your family and friends. Perhaps later in life it will be mostly about your spouse, your children, or a religious community of priests, sisters, or brothers.

3. The call of work

This call addresses the question: "How should I labor?" Right now, the call of work for you is all about school. (Maybe that's why it's called "schoolwork.") But the kind of work you enjoy doing outside of school can sometimes give you a glimpse of how you may want to answer this call when it's time to think about choosing your career.

Each of these calls brings its own set of joys, opportunities, responsibilities, and commitments. And yet, these three vocational calls are always overlapping. How do you know when you are making the right responses to these callings? The answer: when the role lines up with your soul. When and how does the role you play in each of your relationships line up with—agree with—your soul? How about the role you are taking within the call of faith? How and when does it align best with your soul? When and how does your role not agree with your soul? How about the roles you take on in school/work? When and how do they align or not align with your soul?

Sometimes there may be something wrong with the role you are taking within each of your callings, and sometimes there is nothing wrong with the role, but you might need to take better care of your soul. Sometimes your vocational journey will take you to places where these three calls are working together. Sometimes you will find yourself in places where one call may be in tension with another, for example, when the call of faith is in tension with the call of relationships. And sometimes on the vocational journey you will find that one call seems to be written with a capital C, asking you to give it more attention than the other two.

Making spiritual sense

From the time you were little, you've been asked to "develop some common sense" and to "use common sense." But responding to these three vocational callings is a spiritual task that asks you to develop and use your spiritual sense. The spiritual sense with vocations is all about learning to pay attention and address all three calls. It requires that you develop the ability to sense the Spirit's presence in the everyday moments of grace and the everyday challenges you experience in relationships, faith, and work (school).

We Catholics believe that God created us with spiritual sense—that's what it means to be "made in the image of God."

Your Spiritual Sense

Here are some important questions to help you further develop your spiritual sense in terms of callings. These questions are just for you; you don't have to share them with your sponsor or anyone else. Write down your thoughts in the space that follows each question.

When you think about the way you have been responding to the call of faith, the call of relationships, and the call of work:

• To whom or what are you most committed?

• What is being asked of you by this commitment?

• What tensions are you experiencing because of your commitments?

When you reflect on your callings, commitments, and challenges, are there observations you want to make at this time about who you are and whose you are?

But we all tend to bury our spiritual sense beneath all the other stuff pressing in on us. We get caught up in trying to develop all the other abilities we need for life: intellectual, organizational, technological, athletic, musical, social, and mechanical.

Spiritual sense is your ability to catch a glimpse of how the ordinary is sometimes holy and the present is sometimes sacred. Spiritual sense is your ability to evaluate the condition of your three vocational callings and to respond to whatever might need fixing or celebrating. In today's hectic life, only a few people deliberately work on developing their spiritual sense. Everybody prepares for Confirmation, but not everybody starts trying to develop spiritual sensitivity. That's a big part of what this book is trying to help you do.

Stumbling blocks

Some of the obstacles or stumbling blocks to developing spiritual sense about life's callings include:

- The noise of life: too much stuff taking up so much of your attention that you can't "hear" the Spirit's call from above, from within, or in another person's comments. Sometimes the Spirit calls in a way you can't help but notice. But a lot of times the Spirit whispers to our souls— and we can't hear it because of all the noise in our lives.

- Listening to the wrong voices: you might be very open to sensing the Spirit, but you could be counting on the wrong people and the wrong events to show you the way.

- Avoiding the call: sometimes the Spirit is calling you, but for some reason you avoid taking the call—like not answering your phone after checking the caller ID.

- Go to www.spiritandsong.com/compositions/66133 and listen to "Sophia." Check out the Book of Wisdom, chapter 7, to see exactly who Sophia is.

Each call has a "season"

Another helpful way to keep your spiritual sense healthy is to think about your callings in terms of "seasons."

Sometimes within the call of relationships you might feel like you are in Spring, thanks to new friendships or social events. Or you may feel like you are in Fall because some of your relationships are changing like the leaves on the trees. Some relationships might even be ending—like leaves falling off trees. And you could also be in one season or another within your call of faith and the call of work (school). For example, you could be in Summer within the call of faith because you are enjoying the warmth of your spiritual life. You are relaxed and comfortable. Yet at the same time, you may be in Winter within the call of work if school seems hard and cold and frozen in place. Or you might be in the same season within each of the three callings of your life. Get it?

Here's how the "seeing the seasons" of your callings can help you sustain your spiritual sense. If you don't like the weather within one of your vocational callings, remember it's just a season. And the season will change. It always does. The weather will get better.

If your friends are in great seasons and you are not, don't think there is something wrong with you. It's just the weather of your life right now. Have faith. Try taking some delight in the good seasons your friends are enjoying. And stop thinking that you are inferior in some kind of way. And if you are in wonderful, glorious seasons, God bless you. Enjoy your life right now and give thanks! But remember—it's just a season. Don't get depressed or shocked when the weather changes.

You might be thinking, "Can I change the season I'm in?" No, not any more than you can change the real weather. There's a force at work that is bigger than you. It's the Spirit. And it is mystery. Vocational spirituality—and the spiritual sense that comes with it—embraces mystery.

You get to choose how you want to answer the call of faith ("How am I to live?"), the call of relationships ("With whom am I to live?"), and the call of work ("How should I labor?"). It's all about your life. But each of these three calls comes with commitments, challenges, and responsibilities. They also come with wonderful moments of grace to help you make good decisions.

Your Vocational Seasons

Take time now to name the season you are in within each of the three callings. Name the season and explain why you feel this way.

Call of Faith

Season I'm in: _____

Reason(s) I say this:

Call of Relationships

Season I'm in: _____

Reason(s) I say this:

Call of Work (school)

Season I'm in: _____

Reason(s) I say this:

Each of these calls invites you to give of yourself fully to God, to loved ones, and to the work you want to do, and giving yourself can be hard work. So here's the bottom line about vocational spirituality: it's all about your life, but it's not about a life that's all yours.

● Go to www.spiritandsong.com/compositions/10409 to hear a song about how well God knows you.

You have already taken a survey to get a first impression about the strongest and least developed dimensions of your spirituality. You also used faith, hope, and love to see how these dimensions overlap and what comes easiest for you. You even examined the spiritual dimensions of the Ten Commandments.

Talk to Your Parents!

Take time now to ask your parents or guardians the following questions, and write their responses below. (You might want to talk to them about each of the callings, or let them read the previous few pages about the three callings.) Note to sponsors: Interview two friends.

• What season are you in within the call of work? Why?

• What season are you in within the call of faith? Why?

• What season are you in within the call of relationships?

Then we switched gears and looked at the callings you are experiencing and the commitments that come with each of these callings. All of this is designed to help you take a deeper look at your spirituality so you can begin developing your own Spiritual Growth Plan, one that responds to *your* spiritual interests and needs.

- Go to www.spiritandsong.com/compositions/66895 if you are looking for a song to help remind you why your work here is worthwhile.

You have now completed Part One of this process and you have set in place a few basics for your Spiritual Growth Plan on the next two pages. You will add more after Part Two and eventually try to put it all together after Part Three.

Notes

My Spiritual Growth Plan: Part 1

The Three Dimensions of Spirituality

1. Go back to the My Spiritual Life Profile on pages 4–5. Look at your scores. What is the strongest dimension(s) of your spirituality (vertical, horizontal, or internal)?

How strong is it compared to the other dimensions?

What's the least developed dimension of your spirituality and how weak is it compared to your other dimensions?

2. Which statement in the Seeing Three Dimensions exercise on pages 7–10 comes closest to something you might say?

How would you say this in your own words?

3. Which of the Ten Commandments do you feel strongest about?

Is this because it represents your strongest spiritual dimension or your weakest?

4. When it comes to faith, hope, and love, which are you most drawn to?

Based on these reflections, circle the dimension of your spirituality that you want to develop more deliberately.

  vertical   horizontal   internal

How can you begin to do so (see hints below)?

• To strengthen the vertical, invest more time and energy in personal prayer, going to church, and reading the Bible.

• To strengthen the horizontal, give more attention to treating others lovingly, recognizing those in need, informing your conscience and evaluating the moral decisions you make.

• To strengthen the internal, start the deliberate practice of counting your blessings by keeping two minutes of quiet gratitude every day, and also practice sharing your frustrations with God.

Three Vocational Callings

In order to keep developing your spiritual sense, ask yourself:

1. Which calling might the Spirit be asking you to deliberately give more attention to: faith, relationships, or work/school, and why do you think this?

2. What's the most important task you face within that calling right now?

3. With whom can you talk about this in more detail?

Sponsor conversation #1

Please get in touch with your sponsor now and compare notes on the following:

- Which call(s) have you been focusing on the most (faith, relationships, work/school)?

- Which call(s) have you been neglecting?

- What call(s) have you found to be pulling against another?

- In light of all this, what task(s) lie ahead for you?

Also compare notes on the following:

- Your highest and lowest score on the Spiritual Life Profile and whether or not you found these three dimensions of spirituality to be helpful.

- Your responses to Your Spiritual Sense (page 12).

- The spiritual season you are in currently within each one of the three callings: faith, relationships, and work/school.

- The biggest obstacle you face when it comes to developing your spiritual sense (see Stumbling Blocks, page 13).

PART 2

A Full Member of the Catholic Church

As you make your final preparation for full initiation into the Catholic faith through the sacrament of Confirmation, it's important to revisit what it means to call the Catholic Church your spiritual home.

We'll start this section with a story. As you read it, make a list of all the questions being asked. After reading it, jot down your own answers.

The Alien at the Retreat

So this alien shows up at the Confirmation retreat and introduces himself/herself/itself.

"Greetings! I am Alien, sent by my people on planet GOG. Fr. Paul, the one you call 'priest,' said I could question you, but I must depart in twelve minutes exactly."

"That's a crazy good mask you got on!" someone said. "Where'd you get that thing?"

Alien glanced nervously at his/her/its galatical watch. "No time for trivia. I must learn quickly what you Katlicks do in those buildings on Sun-days or Moon-days."

"We're called C A T H O L I C S," someone explained, "and we GO TO M A S S on Sundays and sometimes on Saturdays, but not on Moon-days. We don't have those."

"What do you do at this Mass on the day of the Sun or the Sat?" asked Alien.

"We pray together; we talk to God," someone answered.

"Who is God?"

"God is the Supreme Being," someone explained.

"So the Supreme Being is there in the building at this Mass?"

"Correct," someone replied.

"God is everywhere," said another.

"Everywhere? Even inside your shoes? Even inside the refrigerator over there?"

"Everywhere," someone repeated.

The Alien looked at a young person sitting close to his/her/its webbed feet and asked, "They are teasing me, correct? God is not everywhere. It is not so. Is it? What does God look like?"

"God is invisible," the young person replied.

Alien backed up. "So you talk to someone you cannot see, but you know is everywhere?"

The group nodded.

Alien shook his/her/its one-eyed head. "And what do you Catholics do at this Mass on the day of the Sun or the Sat?"

"We celebrate what Jesus did for us," someone replied.

"Who is Jesus and what did he do for you?"

"Jesus is God's son and he died for us."

"Why did he die for you?"

"So our sins would be forgiven and we could go to heaven."

"What's this thing you call 'sin'? And where is heaven? Why would you want to go there?"

Different members of the group tried to answer Alien's many questions. But it only confused him/her/it more and more. He/she/it was struggling to make sense of it all.

"Let me get this straight. You talk to this God that no one has ever seen, but is everwhere. You say that this Jesus died so that you can go to heaven, which is a place no one has ever gone to visit and come back from. And some of you think it is in the sky somewhere but you are not sure. And you say that this Jesus person died, but then came back, and then left again to be with God. And you celebrate this every day of the Sun or the Sat at the Mass. So, how do you celebrate?"

"We read aloud from the Bible. It's a book that God gave us."

"Fr. Paul gives a talk—we call it a 'homily.'"

"We eat the Body and Blood of Jesus," someone said. "It's a mystery. That's why we go to Mass, to celebrate this mystery."

"Yeah, right, okay. My time is about up. This has been very interesting," said Alien rolling his/her/its eyes toward the ceiling. "Last question, just in case someone on my planet asks: how do you join this Catholic group; what do you have to do?"

"Get baptized," someone called out.

"What's that?"

"Get Fr. Paul to sprinkle water on you," teased another.

"Confess your sins!" someone else replied.

"Read the Bible!" someone added.

"Pray!" another called out.

"Get confirmed with us!" someone said.

"Yeah, we're still getting initiated; stick with us," they smiled.

Fr. Paul returned to the room just as Alien began to leave.

"How'd it go?" he asked. But Alien vaporized before he/she/it could reply.

• **How do you think Alien would have answered? What would he/she/it have said? Write your answer here. What do *you* think is the point of the story?**

What Catholics believe

It's pretty difficult to summarize everything you believe in twelve minutes right off the top of your head! Fortunately, someone has worked on this for you. The Nicene Creed, which dates back to around 450 AD, is the only Christian creed that both Catholics and major Protestant denominations accept. It is the Creed you recite by heart during Mass. Now that you've seen what the kids in the Confirmation class told Alien, here's an exercise for you. Compare the ancient Creed with the words from an anonymous "creed" that reflects the beliefs of our modern culture. Notice how the two creeds differ. One describes all of our Catholic beliefs; the other is very vague and general.

Nicene Creed

We believe in one God,
   the Father, the Almighty,
   maker of heaven and earth,
   and of all that is seen
   and unseen.
We believe in one Lord,
   Jesus Christ, the only Son
   of God, eternally begotten
   of the Father,
   God from God,
   Light from Light,
   true God from true God,
   begotten, not made,
   one in Being with the Father.
Through him all things
   were made.
For us and for our salvation
   he came down from heaven:
   by the power of the
   Holy Spirit
   he was born of the Virgin
   Mary, and became man.
For our sake he was crucified
   under Pontius Pilate:
   he suffered, died, and
   was buried.
On the third day
   he rose again
   in fulfillment
   of the Scriptures;

Modern Creed

I believe in God,
   whose spirit is in everyone
   and everything.

I believe in Jesus, who was a
   son of God.

He taught us the ways of God,
   and they killed him
   because of what he taught.

He has an honored place
   in heaven again, with God.

he ascended into heaven
and is seated at the right hand
of the Father.
He will come again in glory,
to judge the living
and the dead,
and his kingdom will have
no end.

We believe in the Holy Spirit,	I believe in God's spirit,
the Lord, the giver of life,	which is a good force
who proceeds from	in the world,
the Father and the Son.	helping everyone get
With the Father and the Son,	through life.
he is worshiped and glorified.	
He has spoken through	
the prophets.	
We believe in one, holy, catholic,	
and apostolic church.	
We acknowledge one baptism	
for the forgiveness of sins.	
We look for the resurrection	I believe in heaven
of the dead,	where I will see God
and the life of the world	after life.
to come. Amen.	

- What does the modern "creed" leave out regarding God? Jesus? the Holy Spirit? the Church?
- Name one thing you like best about the Catholic Creed.
- Ever wonder why we stand when reciting the Creed during Mass? (And, by the way, have you memorized the Nicene Creed yet?)

Catholics are unique

If you have ever wondered, "What's the difference between Catholics and Christians of other denominations?" you're not alone. First of all, we do have some beliefs in common. For example, we share our faith in Jesus as the Son of God who saved us from sin and enables us to share eternal life in heaven. But here are nine characteristics that are unique to our Catholic tradition.

1. We are eucharistic

We believe that Eucharist is not simply a symbolic reminder of Jesus' sacrifice. We believe it is the real presence of his body and blood. Most other Christians see the Eucharist as a memorial or reminder of Jesus' sacrifice. We see it as his real presence.

2. We are sacramental

You walk into a Catholic Church and dip your hand into "holy water" and make the Sign of the Cross. Then you genuflect before you go into the pew and kneel down. You may look at the gold tabernacle or the body of Christ on the large crucifix hanging by the altar. If it is Advent, you may notice a wreath with four candles at the front of the church. If it is Easter, you will see a large white Paschal candle near the altar. If you attend a baptism, you will see oil, water, and light. We Catholics have our own sacramental language; Catholicism is filled with imaginative signs and symbols. We deliberately use colors, symbols, and actions that speak to us in ways that don't require words.

3. We are a communion of saints

We believe in asking faith-filled friends—those living on earth and those in heaven—to pray for us. This teaching is called the "communion of saints," and every Sunday at Mass we pray these words in the Creed: "I believe in the communion of saints." Sometimes after Mass you might see someone silently praying the rosary or praying before a statue of a saint. Maybe one of your aunts or uncles has a small prayer table at home with a picture of a deceased loved one and a candle. That's because we Catholics believe that we are united—as one family of faith— with those who have died and those who are in heaven.

4. We have shared leadership

In your parish you notice altar servers, readers, parish council members, eucharistic ministers, a priest, perhaps a nun, a director of religious education, maybe a religious brother, a youth minister, Catholic schoolteachers, Knights of Columbus members, coaches, and catechists. Catholicism has a clear organizational structure to which everyone can contribute. We believe in shared ministry. So do almost all other Christian denominations, but not always with the same complexity.

5. We are committed to justice for all

Did you know that both Catholic Relief Services and Catholic Charities serve the poor as much as or more than the American Red Cross? Did you know that our bishops led a national discussion about stopping the nuclear arms race? They did the same thing when our country considered cutting welfare to the poor. And did you know that Catholics are committed to these seven principles of social justice: 1. the life and dignity of the human person; 2. the rights and responsibilities of humans; 3. participation in family and community; 4. preference for the poor and vulnerable; 5. the dignity of work and the rights of workers; 6. the solidarity of the human family; and 7. care for God's creation? A committment to social justice is a central characteristic of the Catholic faith.

6. We are apostolic

Pope Benedict XVI succeeded Pope John Paul II, who succeeded Pope John Paul I, who succeeded Pope Paul VI, who succeeded Pope John XXIII, and so on. That's because Catholicism is apostolic: we can trace our roots right back to the apostles and those who came after them.

7. We are universal

When you go to Sunday liturgy, no matter where you are, you recognize it as the same Mass as the one in your own parish. That's because Catholicism is universal and accepts people from every place and every walk of life. We have a "wide tent" under which each Catholic can focus on their favorite spiritual practices and still be accepted. You want to attend Mass every day? There's room for you. You want to say the rosary? There's room for you. Want Bible study? Got that here as well. Want to serve the poor? Can do that here, too. This built-in acceptance of diverse spiritual interests, devotions, and practices—united under the essential teachings of our faith—makes us unique.

8. We have a positive view of human nature

We know we are flawed and imperfect, but Catholics also believe that each human being comes into the world with the natural ability to sense God's presence in things like truth, beauty, and love. Many other Christian faiths believe that humans come into this world completely flawed—without the God-given ability to sense the Spirit. We believe that although we are born with original sin, we are made in the image of God.

9. We respect both faith and reason

Catholics honor theologians and scholars like Augustine and Thomas Aquinas who have helped us think further about God's will for us and how the Spirit may be leading us in our present age. Catholicism fully accepts the Bible as God's word *and* welcomes ongoing discussion and new insights as well. That's because Catholics believe that faith and reason are partners.

Other Christian denominations, of course, share some of these nine characteristics. For example, many Christian denominations make a consistent commitment to justice or believe that faith and reason are partners. And some denominations have additional spiritual characteristics. But what makes Catholics different is the priority we give all nine of these characteristics. They are central to us, have always been part of our history, and are all interconnected.

Interview Three Believers

Set up interviews, if possible, one with a child, one with someone your own age, and one with an older adult. Ask them the questions, then use the space below to record your interviews.

Person #1

Name:_____ Age:____

What's your favorite Catholic season or symbol? Why do you like it?

For you, what's the best thing about Catholicism?

Person #2:

Name:_____ Age:____

What's your favorite Catholic season or symbol? Why do you like it?

For you, what's the best thing about Catholicism?

Person #3

Name:_____ Age:_____

What's your favorite Catholic season or symbol? Why do you like it?

For you, what's the best thing about Catholicism?

Check the box under persons 1, 2, and 3, if their answers contained any of the nine charactersitics of Caholicism.

	Person	1	2	3
Belief in the real presence of Jesus		☐	☐	☐
Sacramental signs and symbols		☐	☐	☐
Communion of saints		☐	☐	☐
Shared ministries		☐	☐	☐
Commitment to justice		☐	☐	☐
Apostolic		☐	☐	☐
Universal		☐	☐	☐
Positive view of human nature		☐	☐	☐
Faith and reason are partners		☐	☐	☐

Now answer the two questions for yourself.

• What's your favorite Catholic season or symbol and why do you like it?

• For you, what's the best thing about Catholicism?

"I've already had this!"

Catholicism is a rich tradition that requires a great deal of religious education. Over the years, you may have found yourself saying, "I've already had this!" See how many of the following questions you can answer correctly. Use the words in the box to help with your answers. (You won't use all of them, and one or two of the answers you need are not there.)

1. Who is the apostle we refer to as "the first pope"? (10 pts)

2. Write out the five liturgical seasons of the church and put them in order, starting with the four weeks before Christmas. (10 pts each)

3. List the seven sacraments in the order they are most commonly received. (10 pts each)

4. What is your bishop's name? (10 pts)

5. List the seven deadly sins, also called "capital vices." (10 pts each)

6. List the seven corporal works of mercy. (10 pts each)

7. Correctly spell the name of your parish. (5 pts)

8. The church's official headquarters is in what city? (5 pts)

9. What is the name of the church's official headquarters? (5 pts)

10. What is the name that jointly describes the three holy days just before Easter? (10 points)
    Name each of those three days. (10 pts each)

11. Name the Sunday before Easter. (5 pts)

12. Name the Sunday that celebrates the coming of the Holy Spirit. (20 pts)

13. In what town did Jesus grow up? (5 pts)

14. How many apostles did Jesus select, including Judas? (5 pts)

15. Name each of the gospels in the New Testament. (10 pts each)

16. Name the five books of the Jewish Torah (the first five books in the Old Testament). (5 pts each)

17. Name the church council that modernized many of our Catholic ways. (10 pts)

18. Name your parish director of religious education. (10 pts)

19. Name the only United States president who was Catholic. (5 pts)

20. Name a famous person who is Catholic. (5 pts)

21. What is the name of your diocese? (5 pts)

22. What is the correct term for the place in the church where the consecrated hosts are kept? (5 pts)

23. What is Jesus' mother's name? (5 pts)

24. What is the liturgical color of Lent? (5 pts)

25. How many days are there in Lent? (5 pts)

26. What is another name for the Mass? (5 pts)

27. Name the meal where Jesus said "This is my body" and "Do this in remembrance of me." (5 pts)

Total possible points: 500   Your total _____

Eucharistic liturgy	The Vatican	Marriage
Purple	Pentecost Sunday	Leviticus
Shelter the homeless	Exodus	Clothe the naked
Eucharist	Red	Forty
Rome	Triduum	Visit the sick
Peter	Ash Wednesday	Green
Mary	Ordinary Time	Greed
Reconciliation	Mark	Twelve
Second Vatican Council	Lust	Envy
Numbers	Holy Orders	Genesis
Anger	Pride	Deuteronomy
Palm Sunday	Nazareth	Advent
Good Friday	Luke	Gluttony
Matthew	Baptism	Give drink to the thirsty
Christmas	Holy Thursday	Tabernacle
Confirmation	Lent	Anointing of the Sick
John Kennedy	John	Visit the imprisoned
Holy water	Feed the hungry	
Bury the dead	Sloth	

Why go to Mass?

This question is usually followed by another one: "Can't I just pray in my own way every Sunday?" Going to Mass (or celebrating the Eucharistic liturgy) is essential to being Catholic. You go to Mass every weekend in order to *worship, rest,* and *remember.*

Mass helps you remember who you are. Things can get crazy during the week. Stuff happens, lots of stuff, stuff that often has you exhausted by the weekend: the expectations of others, peer pressure, and dramas with your friends, parents, and teachers. Attending Mass on Sunday is like stepping out of the chaos and the noise of life long enough to catch your breath. It's like coming to a balcony and looking down on the dynamics of your daily life long enough to remember who you really are, what your deepest values are, what your heart's deepest longing is, and what's most important to you. Life can "dis-member" you. Going to church on Sunday can "re-member" you to your true and soulful self.

Mass also helps you remember whose you are. You came from God and you will be going back to God. Going to Mass reminds you that life is the gift God gave you and it reminds you of how God wants you to live it. Mass re-members you with Jesus himself in the bread and wine, just as he promised at the Last Supper. There's no other way that does this like the Mass does it. It gives you food for the journey, soul food for your soul's journey.

Mass re-members you, re-connects you, to the all the other people who come to pause from their busy lives, who come to reclaim their soulful promise, to sustain their spirits. It gives you a chance to re-member through the Spirit with all the other people who believe. Mass helps you remember that you are not alone.

This is why we confess our sins together. This is why we listen to God's word in the Scriptures and hear it explained in the homily. This is why we stand up together and recite our Creed by heart. (You do know it by heart, don't you?) This is why we pray the Our Father together and offer one another the gift of peace. This is why we share the sacred meal of Christ's body and blood as one family of God. This is why we remind ourselves as we go back out into the world to "love and serve the Lord."

These are our Catholic ways of remembering, reclaiming, and renewing our beliefs, our particular way of "keeping the Lord's day." It's not just about going to church; it's more about coming to life. That's why it's called a celebration.

So why go to Mass? *Worship. Rest. Remember.*

- Remember who you are, whose you are.

- Re-member with Jesus in the bread and wine.

- Re-member with the others traveling the road of faith.

All this is worth the hour you spend at Mass. It's way deeper than praying on your own and calling it "church."

- Now is a perfect time to go to www.spiritandsong. com/compositions/30953 and listen to "In This Place," which sums up the spiritual meaning of gathering at Mass on Sunday.

Notes

_____

_____

_____

_____

_____

My Spiritual Growth Plan: Part 2

We've talked a lot about Catholicism in Part Two, so this part of your SGP gives you a chance to form your own personal Catholic "K-A-B" plan. Here's what you do:

Divide the circle below into three portions by drawing a large Y.

• Label one portion "**K**" and in this portion list the specific Catholic topics you wish to gain more knowledge about.

• Label one portion "**A**" and list the specific Catholic attitudes you want to develop. (Attitude statements usually include phrases like "increase my appreciation for…" "develop more respect for…" "learn to accept…" "become more sensitive toward…" etc.)

• Label one portion "**B**" and list specific Catholic behaviors you wish to include in your life. (Some of these behaviors can be related to Catholic ways of worship and prayer. Some can be related to a commitment to justice. Some might even be related to the items you wrote in the "K" and "A" portions of the circle.)

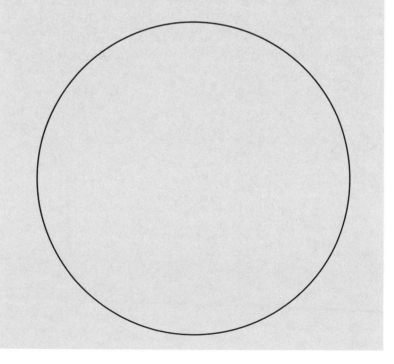

Sponsor conversation #2

Please get in touch with your sponsor and compare notes on the following:

- The point of the parable about "The Alien at the Retreat."

- One thing you like best about the Nicene Creed.

- Your favorite Catholic season or symbol and why you like it.

- One thing you like best about the Catholic faith in general.

- Which of you scored highest on the "I've already had this" exercise?

You have now finished Part Two of this Confirmation process and have added some Catholic knowledge, attitudes, and behaviors to your Spiritual Growth Plan. Let's move on to Part Three!

Notes

_____

_____

_____

_____

_____

_____

Notes

PART 3

After Confirmation

In this final part of the process, you will take a good look at what's possible for your spiritual life as a confirmed Catholic. You may find the expectations high. That's as it should be.

Some people kick back after Confirmation and simply "go with the flow." To be the person God is calling you to be, however, you don't want your spiritual life to drift. More and more in our society, people are pursuing spiritual growth because it can lead to strength, wisdom, and peace. You can acquire these virtues and continue developing your spiritual sense, regardless of what happens after Confirmation, regardless of where you live, what career you choose, or who you choose to spend your life with. Pursue the dream for your soul (soulful dream) that God has planted within you.

Your Soulful Dream

The following exercise is just for you. You are not going to be asked to discuss this with your sponsor or anyone else. Answer the questions with words, initials, or symbols, whichever you prefer.

1. What is your heart's deepest dream? What is it that your heart desires most? How do you see yourself living the life that has been given to you by the Creator? What little dreams make up your heart's deepest dream?

2. People who loved you when you came into this world had you baptized and claimed you for Christ. How are you investing in that "promise to become" the kind of person God intended you to be? What do you need to do more of? less of?

3. What tempts you most to trade in your heart's deepest dream and your spiritual "promise to become"? Feel free to use words or symbols here as well.

- Go to www.spiritandsong.com/compositions/66253 and listen to "Sacred Silence," a song to give you some quiet prayer time.

What "ship" are you in?

Imagine for a second that living your life is like sailing on the ocean. You are sailing in a particular ship in order to reach your heart's deepest dream. Sometimes the water is calm and the weather is warm and life is fun. But sometimes the water is rough and the weather is stormy and life is tense and hard. Now imagine that you can choose to sail in a number of different ships and each has its own particular activities and functions.

Which of the following "ships" listed below best represent the "boat" that you are in most of the time? *Circle* one or two of the "ships" you currently spend your time on as you navigate your way across the ocean toward the fulfillment of your soulful dream. *Underline* the one or two "ships" you wish you could spend more time on, to learn more about. Then make notes about how you might actually and specifically spend more time in the ships you have just underlined.

scholarship	leadership	citizenship	
friendship	stewardship	hardship	
sportsmanship	relationship	worship	kinship

_____

_____

_____

_____

The call of discipleship

The late Pope John Paul II called all Catholics to get on board the ship of discipleship. Over and over again, he reminded us that this is exactly what Jesus called us to do. Our Catholic bishops have talked about this, too, and here's what they said about *you* and discipleship:

> We must offer young people a spiritually challenging and world-shaping vision that meets their hunger for a chance to participate in a worthy adventure....We need concrete ways by which the demands, excitement, and adventure of being a disciple of Jesus Christ can be personally experienced by adolescents—where they tax and test their resources and where they stretch their present capacities and skills to the limits. Young people need to have a true opportunity for exploring what discipleship ultimately involves. (*Renewing the Vision: A Framework for Catholic Youth Ministry*)

A Christian disciple is a person who studies the way of Jesus and commits to following his way. Being a disciple is more than being a believer—way more serious. It's like the difference between people who visit holy places as tourists and those who visit as pilgrims on a pilgrimage.

You are called by God and your Catholic family to live as a disciple of Jesus. This is the "ship" you are asked to sail on after Confirmation. Sailing on the ship of discipleship for the rest of your life is what Pope John Paul II referred to as "the noble adventure."

Here are some of the things discipleship involves:

- strengthening your personal relationship with Jesus Christ and actively working on your ongoing spiritual growth;
- engaging in the practices of personal prayer, worship in the parish, and receiving the sacraments;

- deepening your understanding of the Scriptures and learning how to apply them to everyday life;

- expanding your knowledge of the Catholic tradition, its teachings, and the way they apply to life in today's complex society;

- discerning your vocational callings and what it means to be a contributing member of society;

- paying attention to the justice aspects of current events and upholding gospel principles for peace and justice;

- honoring your parents and contributing to the well-being of your family;

- demonstrating hospitality and respect to those of other faith traditions and cultures;

- prayerfully and honestly examining your moral actions, your decisions, and forming your conscience in light of the gospel and the teachings of the church;

- making service to others a normal part of your lifestyle;

- recognizing the needs of others and responding with your time, talent, and resources.

- Go to www.spiritandsong.com/compositions/66288 and listen to "Just Live It."

What Jesus was taught

When Jesus was young, Mary and Joseph prepared him for his adult journey of faith by making sure he learned the word of God, the traditions of his Jewish faith, the Commandments, and the mitzvot. These are specific actions or activities that reflect the Commandments. Some had to be observed at a cer-

Do Good and Do No Harm

Christian discipleship, like the Jewish mitzvot, shifts you from simply being a good person who "does no harm" to becoming a person who actively seeks to do good. As you think of the noble adventure of discipleship, the one you are called to embrace after Confirmation, place an asterisk by the mitzvot of Jesus that you would also like to add to your own daily practice.

Jesus' words (Hebrew)	Our words (English)
Bikkur Cholim	Visiting the sick
Kibbud Av Va'eym	Honoring your parents
Gemilut Chasdim	Doing acts of loving kindness
Tzaar Baalie Chayim	Being kind to animals
Chesed shel emet	Caring for the dead
Bal Tashchit	Do not destroy
Shemirat Shabbat	Observing the Sabbath
Hiddur P'nai Zaken	Showing hospitality
Hachnasat Kallah	Rejoicing with bride and groom and others at their significant moments
L'Vayat Hamayt	Comforting the sorrowful
I'Yun T'Filah	Praying with sincerity
Va-Hava'At Shalom Bein Adam La-Chavero	Making peace where there is strife
Nedarim	Keeping your commitments
Tzedakah	Giving to eliminate injustice
Hiddur P'nai Zaken	Esteeming the elderly
V'ahavta L'reyacha	Loving your neighbor
Talmud Torah K'neged Kulam	Studying the word is equal to them all

tain time of the day (morning prayer) or a specific time of the year (eating certain foods at Passover). Some were light (celebrating a festival) and some were heavy (learning Hebrew). Some mitzvot were designed to help one's relationships with other people (horizontal), and some were designed to help one's relationship with God (vertical). And Jesus' people believed that doing any mitzvot made a person stronger when it came to handling life's ups and downs (internal).

Jesus was taught that practicing mitzvot was a key component of the adult journey of faith. To the left are a few of the mitzvoth he was taught.

- Go to www.spiritandsong.com/compositions/66129 and listen to "Isaiah 61," which describes Jesus as he announces who he is before the Jewish elders in the synagogue. (You can read about this in Luke 4:17.)

Evaluating my discipleship

Statistics and polls tell us that almost nine out of ten people believe in God, heaven, and hell, and pray regularly. So it seems that the world today does not need more believers. What it does need now are more disciples: believers whose faith shapes the way they live; people who are committed to "act justly, love tenderly, and walk humbly with their God" (Micah 6:8).

Discipleship is challenging and it's hard, but it's real life. It brings real joy as well as real sorrow. It takes real faith, hope, and love. It offers real peace.

Discipleship is a full way of life; it is life the way it is meant to be lived. Are you in? If so, go over each of the eleven tasks of discipleship on the next page and on the line provided rate yourself from 1–5 (with 5 being excellent). Then make a note after each one, describing one positive way you can practice it. For example: "Show Mom more love," or "Thirty min. w/ my Bible Sunday nites," or "Pitch the nasty CDs," or "Try to keep a prayer journal for a month."

Discipleship: Are You In?

_____1. Strengthening your personal relationship with Jesus Christ and actively working on your ongoing spiritual growth.

Notes:

_____2. Engaging in the practices of personal prayer, communal worship, and the sacramental life of the church.

Notes:

_____3. Deepening your understanding of the Scriptures and learning how to apply the Scriptures to everyday life.

Notes:

_____4. Expanding your knowledge of the Catholic tradition, its teachings, and the way they apply to life in today's complex society.

Notes:

_____5. Discerning your vocational callings and what it means to be a contributing member of society.

Notes:

_____6. Paying attention to the justice aspects of current events and upholding gospel principles for peace and justice.

Notes:

_____7. Honoring your parents and contributing to the well-being of your family.

Notes:

_____8. Demonstrating hospitality and respect to those of other faith traditions and cultures.

Notes:

_____9. Prayerfully and honestly examining your moral actions, your decisions, and your conscience in light of the gospel and the teachings of the church.

Notes:

_____10. Making service to others a normal part of your lifestyle.

Notes:

_____11. Recognizing the needs of others and responding with your time, talent, and resources.

Notes:

The word on discipleship

Read the entire Gospel of Matthew: the whole thing. Then list below seven things Jesus says in these chapters about being a disciple. Write out each statement in your own words and include the chapters and verses that correspond to your selections. For example: A disciple should help light the way for others (Mt 5:14). Be prepared to share your selections with your sponsor.

Seven characteristics of discipleship

1.

2.

3.

4.

5.

6.

7.

- Go to www.spiritandsong.com/compositions/30999 and listen to "Be Merciful, O Lord." It will remind you of God's kindness and help you take heart.

Take Heart

You have learned a lot so far in your life—without books like this one. Life itself has taught you a lot. Make a few notes about what you have already "learned by heart," so to speak.

• What have you learned to be true about people?

about yourself?

about God?

• What have you learned about beauty?

• What are some of the most beautiful things you have seen or experienced?

• What have you learned so far about love?

• When and with whom have you felt most loved?

People change when they lose heart. When we lose heart

   our openness becomes suspicion…but we call it maturity.

   our optimism becomes pessimism…but we call it getting smarter.

   our enthusiasm becomes apathy…but we call it taking things in stride.

   our excellence becomes mediocrity…but we call it reality.

Now add a few more similar statements. When you lose heart…

_____becomes _____ but we call it _____.

_____becomes _____ but we call it _____.

_____becomes _____ but we call it _____.

What sometimes causes you to lose heart?

The Spirit brings gifts

As Catholics, we believe that the Holy Spirit offers us gifts to help us live as disciples of Christ. From time to time, you experience these gifts as moments of grace when you need them most and they keep you from losing heart. The Old Testament prophet, Isaiah, listed seven of these gifts (Is 11:2–3):

Wisdom	Understanding	Fortitude	Counsel
Knowledge	Piety	Fear of the Lord	

Look at each of the following situations and name the gift of the Spirit that is either needed or already being used.

• Sheri started smoking out of curiosity, even though she knew that smoking was stupid and that it kills people. But now she can't stop smoking, even though she hates the habit. _____

• Briana and her dad went fishing early in the morning. They heard a noise in the morning fog behind them and turning, they saw three deer silently drinking from the river. For one very long minute they both stared at the deer. Then Briana's dad whispered. "Thank you, God," and went back to fishing. _____

• "If we torture terrorists, then we're as bad as they are!" Bernie shouted over the music. "But what if they're planning to blow up the elementary school or something? Don't we need to stop them? Isn't torture justified if it saves innocent lives?" Jimmy argued. "You just don't torture another human being. It's not right!" Bernie replied. "Maybe sometimes you have to." Jimmy answered.

_____

• "Cool cross." Corina told Carlos as she studied the crucifix he wore around his neck. "My stepfather gave it to me when I turned thirteen," Carlos said. "He told me, 'Now you are a man. Take this cross and wear it; it will remind you to be a good man.' I never take it off."

- "No pressure, but everyone's gonna be there." Mallory announced in the cafeteria during lunch. "No chance for trouble, no parents, just hangin' out with friends." Sharon was thinking about going, but she was nervous. "Why risk it?" her friend Becca asked. "Someone brings something and you get kicked off the team." "Not if I don't drink!" Sharon answered. "Yeah, try explaining that to Coach Kenton and Principal Schmidt." Becca said. "But I really want to go," Sharon sighed. _____

- "Say that again." Richard asked. Phil once again explained how to access the computer files that were not on the desktop or in documents. "Okay. I think I get it. But how do I download from there into my iPod and still burn a CD?" Phil took Richard through the steps of that process too. "How'd you figure this out?" Richard asked. "I dunno; it's just easy for me," Phil answered.

- Jane was riding home from a Friday night ball game with some friends. Her best friend's boyfriend was sitting right next to her in the backseat. He reached out to hold her hand. "Can I kiss you?" he asked quietly.

- The boss called an important meeting on Sunday morning. "I'm sorry, but I can't do business on Sunday," said Eric. "It's against my religion." "But you owe it to the rest of us," replied his boss. "We need you there." "I'm sorry. I just can't work on the Sabbath," said Eric.

- Go to www.spiritandsong.com/compositions/66096 and listen to "Give Me a New Name." What does this song say about why we take a new name at Confirmation?

Your Own Experience

Describe a time when you have recognized a particular gift of the Spirit working within you.

What gift(s) of the Spirit do you need most right now? In what situations do you need it?

Notes

_____

_____

_____

_____

_____

_____

_____

Suffering and discipleship

Questions that often emerge, even from those committed to discipleship, are: How come good things happen to bad people? Why does God allow good people to suffer?

It's true that suffering can sometimes cause you to lose heart. There is no nice way to sugarcoat it. Some religions make it seem that everything will always be easy as long as you are a disciple. Life will always be good. No pain. No tears. No tragedy. No suffering.

But our Catholic faith fully accepts suffering. We don't believe anyone is promised a free pass from suffering. How can we? Not even the perfect one, Jesus, was spared from suffering. In other words, Catholics believe that discipleship comes with a cross. Each person may be asked to bear the cross of suffering at one time or another in life. We don't know why because suffering is a mystery. It's closely tied to the Paschal Mystery, the name we give to the suffering, death, and resurrection of Jesus.

The Paschal Mystery is the summation of Jesus' life and mission and suffering was a key part of it. But so was resurrection. It goes like this:

1. Jesus suffered big time. It made him so scared that he sweated blood. He was falsely accused, stripped naked, beaten, and tortured. He was humiliated, and his mother and friends had to witness all of it.

2. He experienced a horrendous death.

3. Then God raised him from the dead.

It is similar with your own suffering.

1. The pain might be big time. You may be scared, sad, embarrassed, lonely, hurt, or even badly wounded (especially emotionally).

2. Something you love might end or someone you love might leave you. It can feel like a kind of death.

3. But God will help you will get back up and move on to new life.

The Paschal Mystery is a big part of Catholic spirituality. We believe that Jesus' suffering, death, and resurrection can help us deal with our own suffering, death, and new life. And because Jesus suffered for us, we will get through our own suffering. This is the heart of our belief. Our faith won't spare us from pain, but it will definitely help us get through it.

Practically speaking, we believe that every "goodbye" and the sadness that comes with it will be followed by a new "hello." Every ending and the painful loss that comes with it will be followed by a new start. When something dies we will grieve, but then something new will begin. This is what we believe about suffering and this is what we learn from the Paschal Mystery of Jesus.

- Describe an experience of "Paschal Mystery" that you have had and each of its three stages: the suffering, the loss or "death," and the new beginning.

_____

_____

_____

_____

_____

_____

Six skills for discipleship

In Part One, you looked at the three dimensions of spirituality and the three vocational callings of your life. In Part Two, you revisitied what it means to have Catholicism as your spiritual home. And here in Part Three, you have looked at some of the key characteristics of discipleship.

The following six spiritual practices are basic and proven ways of sustaining the spirit throughout your life beyond Confirmation. If you start using these practices, your spirituality will keep growing, even if you just begin with a few small steps.

Dorothy Day, founder of the Catholic Worker movement, put it this way: "The very word 'practice' brings with it the idea of learning. And any practice is awkward and difficult at first. But it is necessary to attain any kind of proficiency in the spiritual life."

Skill #1: Praying all ways

Prayer is like oxygen for your soul. It's how you nurture your Spirit. If you pray only when you need help, it's like nurturing your body only when it's about to faint. But you know this already, right? Most of us get set in our prayer ways and after awhile our practice of prayer gets a little stale. So here are a few suggestions for different ways to pray, ways that will bring "fresh air" to your soul on a regular basis.

You can "TAPP" into God's presence when you pray using this sequence:

Thanksgiving for the blessings you have been given—both big and small.

Admission of your faults—like failing to do good things when you had the chance or the things you wished you hadn't done at all.

Pause long enough for the Spirit to talk back to you. Leave time for listening.

Petition God for what you need, and for the needs of others.

So if you ever want to pray, but aren't sure how to get started, just TAPP.

Lectio Divino (praying with the Bible)

The Benedictine monks are thought to have established this form of prayer. It consists of four actions:

- reading the Word of God,
- thinking about it and digging for its meaning in your life,
- praying about it, responding to God about what the reading says to you,
- contemplation, resting, and listening to the Spirit's response in your soul.

Try this for a few weeks!

Aspirations: prayerful phrases uttered in one breath

You can use these any time you want, at any time of the day, and you can make up your own aspirations—ones that speak to your soul's deepest longings or your heart's deepest dream. Here are some examples:

"Thank you, Lord, for your blessings."

"Lord, help me be more like you."

"God bless us all."

"Guide my steps, Lord."

Write one or two aspirations that you already use, or make up one or two that you can use as prayer from here on out.

1.

2.

Lamentations: a faithful prayer of pain

Lamentations have two parts: 1. an honest expression of emotion like anger, grief, sadness, or frustration, 2. followed by a statement of faith and hope in God's love.

You can practice lamenting for yourself, for another individual's situation, or lamenting for victims of injustice or tragedy. Here's an adaptation of an Old Testament lamentation:

> When I think about my suffering, I feel miserable. And I can't help thinking about it over and over again. I try to remember your great love for me, O God, and that gives me hope. You never stop caring about me. (from Lam 3:19–25).

Write a lamentation here for yourself, someone else, or a group of people experiencing suffering or injustice. Remember: it has two parts.

Formal prayer

This involves reciting memorized prayers, such as the Our Father, Hail Mary, or Apostles' Creed, in order to help you center yourself internally. Formal prayer can also include the practice of devotions like reciting the rosary or praying the Stations of the Cross.

All of these different prayer practices are built on the same foundation. As Catholics, we believe that praying "all ways" consists of three basic dynamics:

conversing with God in a vocal way,

seeking the quiet voice of the Spirit, which we often call meditation,

enjoying the love of God, which we often call contemplation.

Skill #2: Attending to stories

Stories hold truth. The practice of attending to stories is about paying attention to the spiritual truth and wisdom contained in stories people tell while eating lunch or riding in a car together. Spiritual truth and wisdom can be found when you pay attention to the deeper messages found in the stories family members tell, songs you listen to, books you read, and TV shows and movies you watch.

Attending to stories is about deliberately paying attention—investing time and energy—to the stories all around you. When you do this, you will discover truth, wisdom, humor, and encouragement to help you sustain your spirit. Here are some examples of spiritual themes you may find in stories:

Loss	Vulnerability	Blindness
Hope	Power	Labeling
Fear	Hypocrisy	Evil
Love	Redemption	Failure
Pain	Self-doubt	Questioning
Faith	Rejection	Acceptance
Charity	Courage	Honesty
The sacred	Fierce determination	

• What recent song, movie, TV show, newspaper/magazine article, poem, or short story has offered something that sustained your spirit?

• What was the message or spiritual theme that was most helpful?

Skill #3: Keeping company

There is a difference between good friends and friends who are good. The practice of keeping company is about deliberately investing in friendships with people who respect the path of discipleship. Trying to stay on the path of discipleship can be hard. You can get betrayed, misled, disappointed, or just plain messed up. The practice of keeping company is about intentionally staying very connected to people who are good—who understand how discipleship can be hard—and have a way of reminding you that it's still worth it.

- Write down the initials of three people who make up the company you keep.

- Who do you need to quit keeping company with?

Skill #4: Collecting moments of grace

Catholicism teaches that humans come into this world with the natural ability to recognize God in experiences of beauty, love, and truth. The practice of collecting moments of grace is a lot like what Jesus described as "having eyes to see and ears to hear." Collecting moments of grace is about recognizing the spiritual moments God gives you and keeping them in your memory.

The secret to collecting moments of grace is to remember what the monks and mystics of the past taught us: the present is holy and the ordinary is sacred. Collecting moments of grace is really about developing some of that spiritual sense mentioned earlier in this book. Moments of grace show up whenever you see a loving act or hear a loving word spoken from one person to another. Moments of grace show up when you notice a beautiful aspect of creation. Moments of grace also come in those times when you feel inspired or empowered or protected by the Spirit. They are sometimes found in special places where you feel close to God. And moments of grace are also found in those times when you are really grateful for someone in your life.

Collecting moments of grace is the practice of taking note of the Spirit's presence in ordinary as well as extraordinary times of truth, beauty, and love.

• What are some moments of grace you have collected lately? Write a symbol or two to describe them instead of using words if you prefer.

• When has someone else helped you see—and collect—a moment of grace?

Skill #5: Confession

Confession is the courageous practice of examining your thoughts, words, and actions, and admitting your mistakes. As Catholics, we have the powerful sacramental experience of reconciliation, confession. But we can also practice confession in our ordinary, everyday interactions.

The practice of confession comes from the heart. It takes a brave heart, a kind heart, and an honest heart to examine how you are living and loving. Most of the time, confession centers on what we may have done wrong. But sometimes you may want to confess that you simply failed to do a good thing—or a helpful thing—when you had the chance.

Confession is the spiritual practice that all the men and women of the past have used to sustain their spirit. The slogan "Confession is good for the soul" is commonly used because confession frees you to admit your mistakes, move past the guilt, and move forward with a fresh sense of trying to do things better. Confession lightens the burden of your soul's backpack.

• Using symbols or initials instead of words, practice confession now by examining your thoughts and actions and admitting your mistakes. Use the space here to mark what you need to confess.

• When was the last time you participated in the sacrament of reconciliation? When can you do so again?

Skill #6: Honoring the body

Every major religion requires that its disciples practice honoring the body. So it is with Catholicism. As disciples of Christ, we are taught that the body is a temple of the Holy Spirit and a gift from God (1 Cor 6:19–20).

The spiritual practice of honoring the body means showing respect for your body and the bodies of others. *A lot of times we get the first part but forget the second.* Honoring the body also includes being satisfied with the one God gave you. In today's society, there is a lot of attention put on the body. Some of it is positive, like taking care of your body, but some of it is sinful, like using our bodies for recreational sex or harming our bodies with drugs, alcohol, and cigarettes.

Honoring the body becomes more than health and hygiene when you acknowledge that it has spiritual value; we honor our bodies because they are a sacred gift from God.

There are many ways to honor the body. Seven of these can be found in the word "respect."

RESPECT

Give yourself a grade from A to F on each of the points covered below. There's a blank space for this next to each item.

_____ 1. **R**est your body.

_____ 2. **E**xercise to keep your body healthy.

_____ 3. **S**exuality is sacred and each person's body should be treated as holy.

_____ 4. **P**ractice good hygiene.

_____ 5. **E**at properly and pay attention to what you are putting in your body.

_____ 6. **C**lothe yourself modestly and respectfully.

_____ 7. **T**alk about the body with respect. Don't make fun of—or use vulgar language—when talking about someone's body.

- Go to www.spiritandsong.com/compositions/67500 and www.spiritandsong.com/compositions/16812 to listen to "Still Small Voice" and "Go Make a Difference." These songs will give you a better idea of the profound effect that Confirmation has on your life, both now and beyond.

Notes

My Spiritual Growth Plan: Part 3

Post-Confirmation Goals

This book has asked you to do a lot of work. You have looked at nearly twenty topics related to your spirituality, the Catholic faith, and the path of discipleship, which you are about to embrace through the sacrament of Confirmation.

You are now asked to put together your own personal Spiritual Growth Plan for life after Confirmation. Follow these steps.

1. Go to your Spiritual Growth Plan in Part 1 (pages 18 and 19) and fill out the next three items:

• The dimension(s) of my spirituality that I want to work on the most is:

• To make this dimension stronger, I will:

• The vocational calling(s) that I think the Spirit is asking me to give more attention to is:

2. Go to your Spiritual Growth Plan in Part 2 (page 36) and review the knowledge, attitudes, and behaviors (KAB) you wish to develop. Then, in the space provided, confirm those that you still want to make as real goals for yourself after Confirmation.

Knowledge:

Attitudes:

Behaviors:

3. Review what you wrote to yourself in the exercise Your Soulful Dream (page 40). In the space below, make notes to yourself about what it takes for you to keep your heart's deepest dream alive and to fulfill your spiritual promise "to become."

4. Review the Mitzvot Jesus himself was taught (page 44). List the ones that you want to intentionally incorporate into your daily practice.

5. Review how you rated yourself on Discipleship: Are You In? (pages 46–47). In the space below, write down the discipleship tasks that you want to make as your own goals.

6. Review the exercise Take Heart (page 49). Write down what you have learned "by heart."

7. Review the six practices for spiritual growth beginning on page 55. Name three that you want to deliberately work on.

1.

2.

3.

Sponsor conversation #3

Time to meet with your sponsor again! This time compare notes on:

- What mitzvot you would like to make part of your lifestyle (page 44).

- At least three things the Gospel of Matthew said to you about discipleship (page 48).

- Your answers to the questions connected with the practice of Skill #2: Attending to Stories (page 58).

- One significant thing about your final Spiritual Growth Plan (pages 64–65).

- What you have found most helpful about this whole preparation process.